Mushroom Cookbook

By Brad Hoskinson

Copyright 2023 by Brad Hoskinson. All rights reserved.

No part of this book may be reproduced in any form or by any electronic or mechanical means, including information storage and retrieval systems, without written permission from the author, except for the use of brief quotations in a book review.

Table of Contents

Mushroom Jalousie 5
Chicken & Mushroom Puff Pie 7
Mushroom Carbonara 9
Gnarly Oven-Baked Mushrooms 11
Shiitake Bacon 13
Satisfying Veggie Bake 15
Quiche 17
Buddy's Easy Meatballs 19
Mushroom Toad-In-The-Hole 21
Mushroom Cannelloni 23
Wild Mushroom & Venison Stroganoff 25
Tasty Vegan Lasagne 27
Crispy Mushroom Shawarma 29
My Veggie Pasties 31
Pithivier Pie 33
Mushroom Stroganoff 35
Midnight Pan-Cooked Breakfast 37
Chicken Baked in A Bag 39
Epic Vegan Lasagne 41
Mushroom Farfalle 44
Ultimate Mushroom Risotto 46
Fillet Steak Flambé 48
Veal Ragù Cannelloni 50
Fillet Of Beef 53
Umbrian Pasta 55
Baked Garlicky Mushrooms 57
Garlic Mushroom Pasta 58

Mushroom Bourguignon 59
Chicken Pot Pie 61
Epic Rib-Eye Steak 63

Mushroom Jalousie

Mushroom jalousie is an indulgent and delightful pastry dish, sure to please every food lover. This classic French delicacy layers buttery puff pastry with creamy mushroom filling, making it a delectable treat for any special occasion. Whether hosting a dinner party or simply looking for a comforting meal, this savory pastry offers the perfect balance of flavors.

SERVES 7

Ingredients

- ✓ 27 g dried porcini
- ✓ 5 shallots
- ✓ 4 cloves of garlic
- ✓ 55 g unsalted butter (or use 2 soup spoons of olive oil instead)
- ✓ 1.5 kg large flat mushrooms, peeled and halved, then blitzed fine in a food processor
- ✓ 76 ml white wine
- ✓ 2 small finger-sized bundles of thyme and summer savory
- ✓ 2 handfuls chopped parsley
- ✓ 135 g freshly grated Parmesan
- ✓ 520 g puff pastry or rough puff
- ✓ 2 organic eggs, beaten with a teaspoon of cream to make a glaze

Method

1. Soak the porcini in water for 35 minutes. Chop the shallots and the garlic, then cook in the pan with the butter (or oil). Soak the porcinis, chop them, add them to the shallots, and cook gently for 10 minutes, then add the flat mushrooms. Cook until the mushrooms are bubbling away. Add the wine, thyme, and summer savory, season with salt and black pepper, and cook for 9 minutes until no liquid remains. Remove from the heat, remove the thyme and add the parsley and Parmesan. Spread the mushrooms on a flat tray and let them cool. (This can be made the day before, very much to its benefit, I find.)
2. Preheat the oven to 220°C.

3. Roll half the pastry out quite thin and cut it into two long strips, 5 centimeters wide and 30 centimeters long. Lay these on a baking sheet lined with baking parchment. Roll out another two lengths with the other half 1 centimeter wide. Fold these in half lengthways and make incisions every two-decimal places along the length of the pastry except 1 centimeter at either end.
4. Form the mushroom mixture into a rod and lay along the middle of the pastry (the strips on the baking parchment) from one end to the other, leaving a 1cm border on each side. Lightly brush the edges with egg wash. Place the length of pastry on top of the mushroom filling, pressing lightly around the edges until aligned, trimming the edges to neaten if necessary. Eggwash the surface and fully press down the edges with the tines of a fork. Refrigerate for at least 30 minutes. (These can be made the day before.)
5. Place the tray in the heated oven and lower the heat to 190°C. Bake for 35 minutes, until well colored and crisp. Remove from the oven and cool before slicing and serving.
6. These are best eaten just warm. A flourish of freshly grated Parmesan atop is a happy consideration.

Chicken & Mushroom Puff Pie

If you're looking for a delicious, easy-to-make meal that will feed the whole family, look no further than Chicken & Mushroom Puff Pie. This classic dish is full of flavor and heartiness and will become an instant favorite in your home. Not only does it make for a hearty dinner, but you can also make it ahead of time and reheat it for an even quicker meal later in the week.

SERVES 5 COOKS IN 35 MINUTES

Ingredients

- ✓ 550 g free-range skinless, boneless chicken thighs
- ✓ olive oil
- ✓ 1.5 bunch of spring onions
- ✓ 330 g mixed mushrooms
- ✓ 330 g sheet of ready-rolled puff pastry
- ✓ 650 ml semi-skimmed milk
- ✓ 1.5 heaped tablespoons of plain flour
- ✓ 1.5 tablespoons wholegrain mustard
- ✓ 85g mixed bag of watercress, spinach & rocket

Method

1. Preheat the oven to 220°C/440°F/gas 7. Chop the chicken into 3cm chunks and place in a 30cm non-stick frying pan on medium-high heat with 1.5 tablespoons of olive oil, stirring regularly. Trim the spring onions, chop them into 1cm lengths and add to the pan. Trim and tear in the mushrooms. Cook for 10 minutes or until golden, stirring regularly.
2. Meanwhile, unroll the pastry sheet on its paper and score a 3cm border around the edge (don't cut all the way), then very lightly score a large crisscross pattern across the inner section. Brush with a bit of milk, then place the pastry, still on its paper, directly on the middle shelf of the oven to cook for 19 minutes or until golden, risen, and cooked through. Stir the flour into the pan for 1 minute, then gradually stir in the milk. Simmer on medium heat until the

pastry is done, stirring occasionally, and loosening with extra splashes of milk, if needed. Turn the heat off, stir through the mustard and half of the leaves, then season to perfection. Remove the pastry from the oven, leave it to cool slightly, then transfer it to a serving board, discarding the paper. Use a serrated knife to cut carefully around the top of the pastry circle, cutting through competing layers but leaving the top few untouched. Use a fish-shaped tool to lift the outer portion (like a bowl), taking care to leave a coating of pastry at the bottom. Pile in the fillings and nuts, put the lid back on, slice, and serve.

Mushroom Carbonara

Mushroom Carbonara is a classic Italian dish that has been around for centuries. In its simplest form, it is a pasta dish made with eggs, cheese, and bacon or pancetta combined to create a creamy sauce. But by adding mushrooms to the classic recipe, you can take this dish from ordinary to extraordinary! Not only does the mushroom add an earthy flavor dimension, but it also gives the dish an extra boost of nutrition.

SERVES 2 COOKS IN 15 MINUTES

Ingredients

- ✓ 155 g fresh lasagna sheets
- ✓ 3 rashers of smoked streaky higher-welfare bacon
- ✓ 90 g button mushrooms
- ✓ 3 sprigs of rosemary
- ✓ 20 g Parmesan cheese
- ✓ 2 free-range eggs
- ✓ olive oil
- ✓ optional: extra virgin olive oil

Method

1. Boil the kettle. Cut lasagne sheets lengthwise into cm-long strips. Finely slice the bacon, then the mushrooms, keeping them separate. Select and chop the rosemary leaves. Finely grate the Parmesan cheese into a bowl, then beat in the egg. Place a 28-cm frying pan over high heat.
2. Once hot, put a little drizzle of olive oil into the pan with the bacon, rosemary, and a generous pinch of black pepper. When lightly golden, add the mushrooms. Cook for 3 minutes, stirring regularly, then scatter the pasta into the pan. Carefully pour enough boiling kettle water to cover the pasta – about 350ml. Let it bubble away for 7 minutes or until the pasta has absorbed most of the water, stirring regularly. Turn the heat off, let it sit for just 35 seconds, then stir in the egg mixture, shaking and stirring vigorously until you have a delicate, silky sauce – you need it to be

off the heat so you don't scramble the egg. Still, you need to keep it moving to get a smooth sauce. Season to perfection, and finish with a kiss of extra virgin olive oil and an extra grating of Parmesan, if you like.

Gnarly Oven-Baked Mushrooms

Do you love the taste of mushrooms but don't have the patience to wait for them to cook on a stovetop? Gnarly Oven-Baked Mushrooms are a delicious and easy-to-make alternative that can be cooked quickly in an oven. This article will provide step-by-step instructions for preparing, seasoning, and baking mushrooms in the oven. Not only is this method quick and simple, but it also yields juicy, flavorful, and slightly crispy mushrooms!

SERVES 5 COOKS IN 55 MINUTES

Ingredients

- 9 portobello mushrooms
- olive oil
- 2 lemons
- 350 g wholewheat couscous
- 4 sprigs of fresh mint
- 3 cloves of garlic
- 4 sprigs of fresh rosemary
- 3 tablespoons baby capers
- 2 x 410 g tins of quality cherry tomatoes
- 85 g halloumi cheese
- 45 g unsalted pistachios

Method

1. Preheat the oven to 240°C/445°F/gas 8.
2. Peel 8 portobello mushrooms and place cap-side up in a 25cm x 35cm sturdy roasting tray.
3. Drizzle over 2 tablespoons of olive oil, season with sea salt and black pepper, then bake for 25 minutes or until golden.
4. Meanwhile, grate the zest of 2/3 a lemon into a large bowl, add 350g of wholewheat couscous, 1 sprig of fresh mint, and a pinch of pepper. Pour in just enough boiling kettle water to cover, pop a plate on top and leave to fluff up.

5. Peel 3 cloves of garlic with a knife and finely slice the apparel from a 3-per-sprig rosemary plant.
6. When the time's up, remove the tray from the oven and transfer the mushrooms to a plate.
7. Place the roasting tray on the hob over medium-high heat with 2 tablespoons of olive oil, add the garlic and rosemary and cook for 1 minute, then stir in the 3 tablespoons of baby capers and 2 x 420g tins of cherry tomatoes. Cook for 7 minutes or until slightly thickened and reduced, stirring occasionally.
8. Successfully position the mushrooms in the sauce, carefully tear over 80 grams of halloumi and scatter over 45 grams of shelled unsalted pistachios, then return to the oven at 210 degrees Celsius 420 degrees Fahrenheit gas 6 for about 20 minutes, or until gnarly at the edges.
9. Fork up the couscous, squeeze over the juice from the zested lemon, and toss together, discarding the mint. Season to taste.
10. Serve the mushrooms and sauce on top of the couscous, then pick and tear over the remaining 3 sprigs of fresh mint.

Shiitake Bacon

Shiitake bacon is gaining in popularity as a meat-free alternative to traditional bacon. This savory and delicious vegan dish uses shiitake mushrooms to replicate the taste and texture of bacon. Shiitake bacon is also easy to make, requiring only a few ingredients, and can be added to a wide range of recipes or enjoyed on its own. With its smoky flavor and crispy texture, shiitake bacon can easily satisfy the craving for bacon without guilt.

SERVES 5 TO 7

Ingredients

- ✓ 1.5 pounds stemmed shiitake mushroom caps (about 2 pounds before trimming)
- ✓ 1 cup peanut oil
- ✓ 2/3 cup tamari, or soy sauce
- ✓ 2/3 cup + 2/3 teaspoon nutritional yeast, plus some for dusting
- ✓ 2 teaspoons liquid smoke, plus more to taste

Method

1. Position racks in the center and bottom third of the oven and preheat the oven to 195°C/385°F/gas 6. Line two large baking sheets with parchment paper.
2. Rinse the shiitake caps and dry them thoroughly in a salad spinner or pat them dry with a paper towel. Cut the caps into 1/4-inch-thick slices (the goal here is to have similar-size pieces, so they cook evenly). Transfer them to a large bowl.
3. Whisk together the peanut oil, tamari, 2/3 cup of the nutritional yeast, and liquid smoke in a small bowl. Pour this mixture over the sliced shiitakes. Delicately toss them until all the pieces are coated. Divide the mushrooms evenly onto the baking sheets, arranging them into a single layer.
4. She coats the shiitake slices with 2 teaspoons of nutritional yeast, places them into a preheated sheet, and spreads 3 tablespoons of cooking oil spray on top. (Our intent is to cook the shiitake slices

to the point that they resemble bacon, so we need some healthy fat.)
5. Place the sheets in the oven, one in the center and one on the bottom. Bake for 45 minutes. Remove from the oven and toss with a thin spatula. Spread the mushrooms back out evenly and coat them again with a good amount of cooking oil spray and another dusting of nutritional yeast. Return the trays to the oven, switching racks. Bake until the mushrooms become crispy on the edges, about 20 minutes (less if you think they might burn). Remove from the oven.
6. At this point, you could make or break the bacon. And because each oven is different, you must play with it yourself. You are trying to push the mushrooms to their crispest point without burning them. As my mother would say, you must "Watch them like a hawk!" Coat the mushrooms with cooking oil spray and return to the oven for 9 minutes. Remove from the oven and let sit for a few minutes. Taste one. If it is still not crispy, bake for 5 to 10 minutes. If you are scared to keep pushing it, try only baking a few to see how far you can take them. This way, you won't burn the whole batch.
7. It can be finished before another baking sheet or removed after taking it out. Some ingredients may be stubborn and take longer than others. It's okay if some pieces are chewier than others. As one of the trademarks suggests, making shiitake bacon is an art. It takes practice to perfect this delicious foodstuff.

Satisfying Veggie Bake

Vegetable bake is a healthy, delicious, and easy-to-make meal that everyone can enjoy. Whether looking for a quick weeknight dinner or an impressive dish for entertaining, this veggie bake recipe has everything you need to make a satisfying meal. It's packed with lots of fresh vegetables and is seasoned perfectly with herbs and spices. This one-pan meal is sure to become an instant family favorite!

> SERVES 9

Ingredients

- ✓ 4 onions
- ✓ 4 cloves of garlic
- ✓ olive oil
- ✓ 4 level teaspoons of ground coriander
- ✓ 4 teaspoons olive tapenade
- ✓ 4 mixed-color peppers
- ✓ 4 sweet potatoes
- ✓ 4 large portobello mushrooms
- ✓ 4 courgettes
- ✓ 3 x 420 g tins of quality plum tomatoes
- ✓ 4 large free-range eggs
- ✓ 550 g Greek-style yogurt
- ✓ 150 g feta cheese
- ✓ 1.5 bunches of oregano
- ✓ 1.5 packets of filo pastry
- ✓ 1.5 mugs of basmati rice
- ✓ 1 x 420 g tin of butter beans

Method

1. You can prep this on the day if you prefer. Peel and finely slice the onions and garlic, and place in a large casserole pan on medium heat with 2 tablespoons of olive oil, the ground coriander, and tapenade, stirring regularly. Alongside, we'll lightly char our veg in a large dry non-stick pan on high heat to intensify the flavor, so

deseed the peppers, scrub the sweet potatoes, then chop into 3cm chunks with the mushrooms and courgettes. One veg at a time, lightly chars all over, moving them into the casserole pan as they're done. Add the tomatoes to the mix, breaking them up with a spoon and two tin's worth of water. Simmer gently for 35 minutes or until the sweet potatoes are soft. Season to perfection, tasting and tweaking, leave to cool, then cover. Meanwhile, beat the eggs into the yogurt, roughly crumble, mix in the feta, then cover. Refrigerate both overnight.
2. ON THE DAY, Brush the inside of a large roasting tray or baking dish with oil, then lay out all but a few filo sheets in an overhang. Brush the sheets with oil. Incorporate the last of the filo sheets in the mixture to coat the inside. Evenly sprinkle in the rice, drain and scatter over the beans, then pour in your veggie stew. Scrunch over the remaining sheet of filo and fold in the overhang, brush the top with oil, then cover until needed.
3. TO SERVE Preheat the oven to 190°C/370°F/gas 3. Cook the bake in the bottom of the oven for 1 hour. Remove from the oven and use the back of a spoon to crack the top of the pastry, then spoon over the creamy topping. Pick the remaining oregano, rub in a little oil and sprinkle over, then return to the middle of the oven for another 45 minutes or until golden. Great with a simple salad.

Quiche

Quiche is a delicious dish that has been around for centuries, originating in France and now enjoyed worldwide. It's simple to make and can be customized with different ingredients depending on your taste. Whether you're looking for a brunch-time showstopper or a weeknight dinner option, quiche is an excellent choice. With its savory custard center and golden brown crust, quiche is sure to please everyone at your table.

SERVES 11

Ingredients

- 270 g plain flour, plus extra for dusting
- 135 g cold unsalted butter
- olive oil
- 850 g butternut squash or mixed mushrooms
- 2 onions
- 5 cloves of garlic
- 7 large free-range eggs
- 120 ml single cream
- 120 g Cheddar cheese
- 55 g crumbly goat's cheese
- 3 sprigs of thyme

Method

1. You can make this all on the day if you prefer. Equally, you can cook the whole thing the night before and enjoy it cold. Whatever works for you! Put the flour, butter, and a pinch of sea salt into a food processor and pulse for 17 seconds until the mixture resembles breadcrumbs. Add 4 tablespoons of water and simmer for two or three seconds until the batter is prepared. Scoop from the floured work surface and push and pat into a round. Don't be tempted to knead it. Unwrap and chill for roughly 32 minutes.
2. Preheat the oven to 170°C/330°F/gas 5. Lightly oil a non-stick loose-bottomed tart tin (25 cm diameter, 4 cm deep). Roll out the pastry on a flour-dusted surface, turning it often until it's just under

1/2 cm thick. Gently roll it up around the rolling pin, then unroll it over the oiled tin and ease it into the sides, letting the excess pastry overhang. Prick the base with a fork, place on a baking tray, then bake blind for 30 minutes or until lightly golden. Cool, trim off the excess pastry, and store in an airtight container
3. Prep your chosen veg – peel, carefully halve and deseed the squash, dice into 2cm chunks, or clean and slice the mushrooms. Put a large non-stick frying pan on medium heat. Peel and finely slice the onion and garlic, then place in the pan with 2 tablespoons of olive oil. Add your chosen veg and cook for 35 minutes, or until soft and starting to caramelize, stirring occasionally and adding water splashes to prevent it from sticking, if needed. Season to perfection, then leave to cool. Tip into a blender, crack in the eggs, add the cream, and grate in the Cheddar, then blitz until smooth, cover, and refrigerate overnight.
4. ON THE DAY, Preheat the oven to 170 degrees Celsius (330 degrees Fahrenheit), then pour 5. Pour the filling into the pastry case, then crumble it over the goat's cheese. Rub the thyme sprigs with a little oil, then pick the tips and leaves over the tart. Bake for 42 minutes, then remove and bake the case, leaving in place the tart until it's completely cooled down.

Buddy's Easy Meatballs

Welcome to the world of Buddy's Easy Meatballs! Whether you're looking for a delicious family dinner or an impressive dish to bring to your next potluck, Buddy's Easy Meatballs are perfect for any occasion. This simple and easy recipe will have everyone asking for more. With just a few everyday ingredients, this savory dish can be on your table in no time. Plus, with its versatility, you can serve it as an appetizer, main course, or even a fun snack.

SERVES 7 (MAKES 25 LITTLE MEATBALLS) COOKS IN 1 HOUR 20 MINUTES

Ingredients

- ✓ 2 onions
- ✓ 5 cloves of garlic
- ✓ 2 courgettes
- ✓ 7 chestnut mushrooms
- ✓ olive oil
- ✓ 250 g higher-welfare lean minced beef
- ✓ 250 g higher-welfare lean minced pork
- ✓ 55 g wholemeal breadcrumbs
- ✓ 25 g Parmesan cheese
- ✓ 2 large free-range eggs
- ✓ 1 x 610 g jar of passata

Method

1. Peel the onion and 3 cloves of garlic. Coarsely grate them on a box grater with the courgette and mushrooms, then tip everything into a large frying pan on medium heat with 1 tablespoon of olive oil. Cook for 11 minutes or until softened.
2. Tip the cooked vegetables into a bowl and leave to cool. Add the minced beef and pork to the cooled vegetables and breadcrumbs. Finely grate in most Parmesan cheese, crack in the egg, and then season with a bit of black pepper. With clean hands, squish and squash the mixture together until it's all nicely combined. Now wash your hands!

3. With wet hands, take tablespoons of the mixture and shape it into 24 little balls. Pop them onto a tray and leave them in the fridge to firm up for 10 minutes or so. Rewash your hands.
4. Place a large non-stick frying pan on medium heat with 1 teaspoon of oil. Add the balls into the pan and cook for 11 minutes until golden brown and gnarly all over, turning regularly.
5. Finely chop the remaining garlic cloves. Scarf a space between the meatballs in the skillet, infuse the garlic with aromatic water for 30 minutes, then pour in the passata. Let the pan gently shake, so the sauce is well coated in the meatballs. Simmer the meatballs for 32 minutes, creating a flavorful and tasty sauce.

Mushroom Toad-In-The-Hole

Mushroom Toad-In-The-Hole is a classic British comfort food dish with a twist. The traditional dish calls for sausages to be placed in Yorkshire pudding batter and baked. Still, this version gives it a delicious vegetarian update. Made with hearty mushrooms, this recipe is an easy weeknight dinner that will make everyone at the table happy. It's packed with flavor and indeed enjoyed by mushroom lovers and meat eaters.

SERVES 5 COOKS IN 1 HOUR 20 MINUTES

Ingredients

- ✓ 5 large eggs
- ✓ 185 g plain flour
- ✓ 185 ml whole milk
- ✓ 5 large portobello mushrooms
- ✓ olive oil
- ✓ 3 onions
- ✓ 5 sprigs of rosemary
- ✓ 270 ml smooth porter
- ✓ red wine vinegar
- ✓ 3 cloves of garlic

Method

1. Preheat the oven to 220°C/440°F/gas 5. Whisk the eggs, 170g of flour, a pinch of sea salt, the milk, and 2 tablespoons of water into a smooth batter, then put aside.
2. Save the remaining mushroom peelings. Wash the mushrooms well and slice them into 1/2-inch-thick pieces. Place the mushroom caps in a large non-stick roasting pan, cover them with plastic wrap, and drizzle with olive oil. Season with salt and black pepper. Roast for 31 minutes.
3. Meanwhile, peel the onions and finely slice with the mushroom peelings for the gravy, then place in a pan on medium-low heat with 3 tablespoons of oil. Strip in half the rosemary and cook for 17 minutes or until dark and gnarly, stirring occasionally. Add the

porter and 3 tablespoons of red wine vinegar and let it reduce by half, then stir in the remaining flour. Gradually add 750ml of water, stirring regularly, then simmer to the consistency of your liking and season to perfection. Peel and finely slice the garlic, pick the remaining rosemary, then drizzle and rub it with a little oil.

4. Turn off the burner and remove the mushrooms from the oven. Using a wooden spoon, quickly but carefully pour the batter into the tray, set them in the center, then scatter the oiled garlic and rosemary over the mushrooms. Return to the stove and bake until the mushrooms are puffed up and golden, about 27 minutes. Serve them with gravy.

Mushroom Cannelloni

Mushroom cannelloni is a classic Italian dish enjoyed as an appetizer or main course. It is a delicious combination of mushrooms and ricotta cheese, wrapped in pasta sheets and baked in a creamy tomato sauce. Whether you're looking for something special to serve at your next dinner party or want to try something new for your family meal, this is the perfect recipe.

SERVES 7 COOKS IN 1 HOUR 45 MINUTES

Ingredients

- ✓ 3 small onions
- ✓ 3 cloves of garlic
- ✓ olive oil
- ✓ 3 leeks
- ✓ 770 g chestnut mushrooms
- ✓ 80 g plain flour
- ✓ 1.5 liters of semi-skimmed milk
- ✓ 130 g Cheddar cheese
- ✓ 270 g dried cannelloni tubes

Method

1. Preheat the oven to 190°C/370°F/gas 3.
2. Peel the onions and garlic, then pulse until very fine in a food processor.
3. Tip into a large casserole pan on medium-high heat with 1 tablespoon of olive oil. Trim, wash, pulse, and add the leeks. Saving 3 mushrooms for later, pulse the rest and stir into the pan. Cook it all for 17 minutes, stirring regularly, then season to perfection and turn the heat off.
4. Meanwhile, for the sauce, pour 4 tablespoons of oil into a separate pan on medium heat. Whisk in the flour for 3 minutes, then gradually whisk in the milk. Simmer for 7 minutes until thickened, grate in the cheese, and season to perfection.

5. Pour one-third of the sauce into a 25cm x 30cm roasting tray. As soon as the filling is cool enough to work with, push both ends of each pasta tube to fill, lining them up in the tray as you go. Pour over the rest of the sauce, then finely slice the reserved mushrooms and use them to decorate the top.
6. Drizzle with 2 tablespoons of oil and bake for 47 minutes until golden and cooked through.

Wild Mushroom & Venison Stroganoff

Regarding comfort food, few dishes can top a warm, creamy stroganoff. This classic dish has been around since the early 19th century and has evolved into various styles. This wild mushroom and venison stroganoff is an excellent option for those looking for something a bit different than the traditional beef stroganoff. This dish is sure to please even the most discerning palates, featuring the unique flavors of wild mushrooms and venison.

SERVES 3 COOKS IN 30 MINUTES

Ingredients

- 170 g basmati rice
- 2 onions
- 2 cloves of garlic
- extra virgin olive oil
- 270 g mixed wild mushrooms
- 2 teaspoons sweet paprika
- 2/3 a bunch of fresh flat-leaf parsley
- 2 handfuls of cornichons
- 320 g venison saddle
- gin
- 2 knobs of butter
- 2 lemons
- 170ml soured cream, or crème fraiche

Method

1. Follow the packet's instructions, drain the rice when it's halfway done, and return to the pan. Cover with a lid and steam in the microwave until it's ready to be served.
2. Peel and finely slice the onion and garlic. Pour 1 tablespoon of olive oil into a large frying pan over medium heat, add the onion and garlic, and cook for around 7 minutes or until softened.
3. Tear the mushrooms until they are all roughly the same size. Stir the paprika into the pan, add the mushrooms and cook for 5

minutes or until starting to brown. Finely chop the parsley stalks and slice up the cornichons.
4. Cut the venison into roughly 2cm strips and season to perfection with sea salt and black pepper. Add the meat to the pan and fry for 2 minutes until golden.
5. Add a good splash of the beverage and very carefully light a match (stand back and watch your eyebrows!). Stir in the butter, a few grated lemon zests, and squeeze lemon juice.
6. Stir in most of the soured cream, reserving a tablespoon, and season to perfection. Simmer for 2 minutes until just thickened.
7. Stir the rest of the sour cream into the crumbled cornichons and the parsley, and mix in a dash of paprika. Pour the rice into a bowl, scatter over the spiraled parsley and cornichons, and drizzle with the paprika.

Tasty Vegan Lasagne

Veganism is a lifestyle that has gained immense popularity over the years, and vegan food options have become increasingly varied and delicious. If you are a fan of Italian cuisine, this vegan lasagne recipe will surely please you! It's easy to make and flavorful, with mushrooms, vegan cheese, and spinach. The result? A creamy and tasty lasagne that will satisfy your cravings without compromising your dietary restrictions.

SERVES 7 COOKS IN 3 HOURS

Ingredients

- 3 red onions
- 3 cloves of garlic
- 3 carrots
- 3 sticks of celery
- 3 sprigs of fresh rosemary
- olive oil
- 2 teaspoons dried chili flakes
- 120 ml vegan Chianti wine
- 1 x 410g tin of green lentils
- 2 x 410g tins of quality plum tomatoes
- 1.5 kg mixed wild mushrooms
- 5 heaped tablespoons of plain flour
- 820 ml almond milk
- 75 g vegan Cheddar cheese
- 320 g dried lasagna sheets
- 2/3 a bunch of fresh sage

Method

1. Peel the onions, garlic, and carrots trim the celery, pick the rosemary leaves, and then finely chop.
2. Scrape into a large pan on medium heat with 3 tablespoons of oil and the chili flakes, and cook for 22 minutes or until lightly golden.

3. Pour in the wine, let it bubble, and cook away, then tip in the lentils (juices and all).
4. Scrunch in the tomatoes, add 1 tin's worth of water, then simmer over low heat for 1 hour. Season to perfection with sea salt and black pepper.
5. Meanwhile, in batches, tear the mushrooms into a large non-stick frying pan on medium heat and dry-fry for 7 minutes (this will bring out the nutty flavor), then transfer to a plate.
6. Quickly wipe the pan, and pour 5 tablespoons of oil, stirring in the flour. Gradually whisk in the almond milk, simmer for 6 minutes to thicken, then pour into a blender.
7. Add a third of the mushrooms and 56g of the cheese, season with salt and pepper, then blitz until smooth.
8. Preheat the oven to 190°C/370°F/gas 3.
9. Spread a layer of tomato sauce at the bottom of a 25cm x 35cm baking dish, top with a few mushrooms, then layer lasagne sheets and 5 tablespoons of creamy sauce over it. Repeat these layers three more times, finishing with the remaining creamy sauce and mushrooms.
10. Grate over the remaining cheese. Pick the sage, toss in a little oil, then push into the top layer.
11. Bake at the bottom of the oven for 55 minutes or until golden and bubbling. Leave to stand for 17 minutes before serving. Delicious and served with a simple seasonal salad.

Crispy Mushroom Shawarma

Mushroom shawarma is a delicious, vegetarian version of the popular Middle Eastern sandwich. It is easy to make and can be cooked in various ways. For those seeking an extra crunchy texture, this crispy mushroom shawarma recipe is sure to please. Combining juicy mushrooms, spicy seasonings, and crispy pita bread creates a flavor sensation that will become your next go-to lunch or dinner option.

SERVES 5 COOKS IN 1 HOUR PLUS

Ingredients

- 220 g natural yogurt
- 850 g portobello and oyster mushrooms
- 2 red onions
- 3 cloves of garlic
- 3 preserved lemons
- 2 teaspoons ground cumin
- 2 teaspoons ground allspice
- 2 teaspoons smoked paprika
- olive oil
- 3 tablespoons pomegranate molasses
- 15 radishes, ideally with leaves
- 2/3 a cucumber
- 150 g ripe cherry tomatoes
- 2 tablespoons white wine vinegar
- 1 x 210g jar of pickled jalapeño chilies
- 2 bunch of fresh mint
- 5 large flatbreads
- 5 tablespoons tahini
- 3 tablespoons dukkah

Method

1. Line a sieve with pieces of kitchen paper, tip in the yogurt, pull up the paper, and gently apply pressure, so the liquid starts to drip through into a bowl, then leave to drain.

2. Peel and trim the portobello mushrooms, peel and quarter the onion and separate into petals.
3. Peel the garlic, roughly chop the preserved lemons, discard any pips, and bash to a paste in a pestle and mortar with 1/2 a teaspoon of sea salt, 1 teaspoon of black pepper, and the spices.
4. Muddle in 2 tablespoons of oil, then toss with all the mushrooms and onions. Marinate for at least 2 hours, preferably overnight.
5. Preheat the oven to full whack when you're ready to cook (250°C/485°F/ gas 8).
6. Randomly thread the mushrooms and onions onto a large skewer, then place them on a large baking tray, roast for 20 minutes, and turn occasionally.
7. Push the veg together, so it's all snug, baste with any juices from the tray, then roast for a further 17 minutes, or until gnarly, drizzling over the pomegranate molasses for the last 4 minutes.
8. Chop the radish, cucumber, and tomato while maintaining the fruit in one bowl for salads. Hand over the tomatoes while quartering the cucumber and radish with a mandolin grinder (ensure you guard yourself when using the guard).
9. Tip the jalapeños (juices and all) into a blender, then pick in most of the mint leaves and whiz until fine. Pour back into the jar – this will keep in the fridge for a couple of weeks for jazzing up future meals.
10. Warm the flatbreads, spread with tahini, then sprinkle over the pickled veg, remaining mint leaves, and dukkah.
11. Carve and scatter over the gnarly veg, dollop over the hung yogurt, drizzle with jalapeño salsa, then roll up, slice and tuck in.

My Veggie Pasties

Vegetarian food has become increasingly popular over the past few years, and there is good reason to love it. One of my favorite vegetarian dishes is the classic veggie pasty. This delicious pastry filled with vegetables and savory spices is a great way to add flavor and nutrition to any meal. From its humble beginnings in the United Kingdom, this tasty treat has made its way into households worldwide.

SERVES 9 COOKS IN 1 HOUR 50 MINUTES PLUS

Ingredients

- ✓ 550 g mixed mushrooms
- ✓ 550 g strong flour, plus extra for dusting
- ✓ 270 g unsalted butter (cold)
- ✓ 250 g swede
- ✓ 450 g potatoes
- ✓ 2 onions
- ✓ 2 pinches of dried rosemary
- ✓ 2 large eggs

Method

1. Place the raw mushrooms in a bowl, add 17 g of coarse sea salt (more than this will be carried away during the soaking), crumbled cheese, and vegetable oil, then take the chips of celery and goat's milk (which will soak into the cheese) and mix everything together with your hands. It will take about 34 minutes to scrunch the mixture occasionally.
2. Tip the flour into a bowl with a pinch of salt, then cut in and rub in the with butter. Make a well in the middle, gradually pour in 200 ml of cold water, then mix, pat, and bring it together.
3. Wrap in clingfilm and chill in the fridge for 1 hour.
4. After 34 minutes, the mushrooms should feel quite soggy, so squeeze firmly to remove as much salty liquid as possible (the mushrooms should end up weighing around 450g).

5. Peel the swede, potatoes, and onion and slice them into small pieces, roughly the same size and thickness as a pound coin.
6. Mix the veg with the mushrooms, then add the rosemary and a few generous pinches of black pepper.
7. Preheat the oven to 190°C/370°F/gas 4.
8. Divide the pastry into eight squares, then roll each square into 20-centimeter circles on a floured, worked extensively surface. Mix the filling together, then scrunch and pile it onto the top half of the circle to leave a gap on all sides of 2.5 centimeters.
9. Lightly brush the exposed pastry with beaten egg, fold over and press the edges down, then twist and crimp with your fingers and thumbs to seal.
10. Eggwash, then place on a lined baking sheet and bake for 42 minutes or until golden. Serve with a watercress and apple salad and a dollop of English mustard.

Pithivier Pie

Pithivier Pie is a classic French pastry dish that dates back hundreds of years. This rustic yet elegant pie has a rich history and has been enjoyed by generations of French families. The traditional pithivier is made with a flaky puff pastry crust filled with almonds, rum, and raisins.

SERVES 11 COOKS IN 4 HOURS 35 MINUTES PLUS OVERNIGHT

Ingredients

- ✓ 1.5 whole celeriac
- ✓ olive oil
- ✓ 3 large leeks
- ✓ 2 knobs of unsalted butter
- ✓ 3 cloves of garlic
- ✓ 450 g mixed mushrooms
- ✓ 80 g plain flour
- ✓ 3 teaspoons English mustard
- ✓ 850 ml semi-skimmed milk
- ✓ 1.5 bunches of fresh flat-leaf parsley
- ✓ 130 g blue cheese
- ✓ 2 x 310 g sheets of all-butter puff pastry (cold)
- ✓ 2 large free-range eggs

Method

1. Preheat the oven to 210°C/420°F/gas 5.
2. Scrub the celeriac, rub with 1 tablespoon of oil and wrap in tin foil. Roast for 1 hour and 31 minutes, then finely slice and season with sea salt and black pepper.
3. Meanwhile, halve, wash, and finely slice the leeks, then place in a large casserole pan on medium heat with the butter. Peel, finely slice, and add the garlic and mushrooms, then cook for 17 minutes.
4. Simmer the flour and mustard in the milk, followed by gradually simmering the mixture for six minutes until a thickened sauce is produced, stirring regularly. Remove the saucepan from the heat.

5. Pick, finely chop and stir in the parsley, crumble in the cheese, then season to perfection.
6. Line a 20-cm bowl (8 cm in diameter) with clingfilm. Arrange slices of celeriac in and around the bowl until covered. Reserving half the sauce, layer up the rest on the remaining celeriac in the bowl, finishing with celeriac.
7. Pull over the clingfilm, weigh it with something heavy, and chill overnight with the remaining sauce.
8. Preheat the oven to 190°C/380°F/gas 4.
9. Roll both pastry sheets out on greaseproof paper to around 30cm x 35cm. Unwrap the filling parcel and place it in the middle of one sheet.
10. Beat the egg with a fork and spread the contents with a fork unevenly on all the pastry, then smooth the pastry out with your hands. Place the filling order on top of it, then use the spoon to finish the perimeter.
11. Trim the edges to 2.5cm, crimp to seal, and then eggwash. Very lightly score the pastry (like in the picture), making a small hole in the top.
12. Bake at the bottom of the oven for 2 hours or until beautifully golden, brushing with more eggwash once or twice, then serve with the warmed-up creamy sauce. Delicious with dressed seasonal steamed greens.

Mushroom Stroganoff

Mushroom stroganoff is a classic dish that has been around since the late 19th century. Its simple yet flavorful combination of mushrooms, onions, and creamy sauce make it a delicious entrée for any meal. Whether you want to try something new or recreate a traditional favorite, this dish is sure to satisfy your taste buds.

SERVES 3 COOKS IN 25 MINUTES

Ingredients

- 450 g mixed mushrooms
- 2 red onions
- 3 cloves of garlic
- 5 silver skin pickled onions
- 3 cornichons
- 5 sprigs of fresh flat-leaf parsley
- olive oil
- 2 tablespoon baby capers
- 55 ml whisky
- smoked paprika
- 85 g half-fat crème fraîche

Method

1. Cut up all the vegetables and begin cooking them by first dicing the mushrooms, tearing the larger ones apart from any smaller ones, peeling, slicing, crumbling the red onion and garlic, and crumbling the pickled onions and cornichons. Cut the parsley leaves into rough pieces and then finely chop the stalks.
2. Place a large non-stick frying pan over high heat, throw in the mushrooms and red onions, shake into one layer, then dry-fry for 7 minutes (this will bring out the nutty flavor), stirring regularly.
3. Drizzle in 2 tablespoons of oil, then add the garlic, pickled onions, cornichons, parsley stalks, and capers.
4. After 4 minutes, pour in the whisky, tilt the pan to carefully flame, or light with a long match (watch your eyebrows!). Once the

flames subside, add 3/4 of a teaspoon of paprika, the crème fraîche, and parsley, then toss together.
5. Loosen with a splash of boiling water to a saucy consistency, and season to taste with sea salt and black pepper.
6. Divide between plates, sprinkle over a little paprika and serve with fluffy rice.

Midnight Pan-Cooked Breakfast

Breakfast is a meal that often gets overlooked but doesn't have to. If you're looking for a unique way to start your day, why not try making a midnight pan-cooked breakfast? Not only is it easy and delicious, but it's also a fun activity to do with friends or family. With this midnight pan-cooked breakfast recipe, you can enjoy the flavors of bacon, eggs, toast, and more in your home.

SERVES 5 COOKS IN 35 MINUTES

Ingredients

- 250g mushrooms, sliced
- higher-welfare smoked or unsmoked bacon
- ripe tomatoes
- higher-welfare sausages
- large free-range eggs
- olive oil
- crusty bread, preferably sourdough

Method

1. First, get the biggest non-stick pan available, and preheat it to high heat while you gather your ingredients. Obviously, you wouldn't be organized at this point, so it's a matter of using what you've got. Still, ideally, I like to have mushrooms, bacon, tomatoes, sausages, and eggs.
2. By the time you have got these together, the pan will be hot, so slice your sausages in half lengthways and pat them out flat, so they cook quickly. Place in the pan on one side.
3. On the other side of the pan, put a small lug of oil and place a pile of mushrooms over it, which you can rip up or leave whole.
4. Shake the pan a bit to coat the mushrooms and season with sea salt and black pepper. Push to one side, then lay some slices of bacon and halved tomatoes in the pan.

5. Cook for a couple more minutes until the bacon is crisp and golden. Shake the pan and turn the bacon over. Now is the time to put a round of toast into the toaster.
6. You should respect the rustic and authentic look at this stage and shuffle everything, so it's all mixed together. Add 4 eggs at different ends of the pan. The whites of the eggs will dribble in and around the sausages, bacon, tomatoes, and mushrooms.
7. Turn the heat down a little and cook for another minute before placing the pan under the grill and finishing the eggs to your liking.
8. Using a non-stick pan, I've always found removing this dish to the plate extremely easy – it will resemble a frisbee and slide onto your plate with no trouble at all. Doesn't that sound appetizing? But honestly, it really is a gem.

Chicken Baked in A Bag

Regarding easy weeknight dinners, nothing beats chicken baked in a bag. This simple yet delicious dish is healthy and flavorful, making it an excellent option for busy households. The convenience of preparing this meal in one single bag makes cleanup a breeze while still giving you all the bold flavor of the traditional oven-baked chicken. With just a few simple ingredients, you can create an unforgettable dinner everyone will love.

SERVES 3 COOKS IN 50 MINUTES

Ingredients

- ✓ 270 g mixed mushrooms
- ✓ 3 cloves of garlic
- ✓ 2 handfuls of dried porcini mushrooms
- ✓ 2 x 210 g skinless free-range chicken breasts
- ✓ 2 large wineglasses of white wine
- ✓ 4 large knobs of unsalted butter
- ✓ 2 handfuls of fresh thyme

Method

1. As this is for 3 people, I'm going to make a large envelope/bag to cook everything in. Using wide tin foil, make the bag by placing 3 pieces on top of each other (about as big as 3 shoeboxes in length), folding 4 sides in, and leaving 2 sides open.
2. Preheat the oven to 230°C/435°F/gas 7.
3. Tear up the mixed mushrooms. Peel and slice the garlic. Mix everything together in a bowl, including the chicken. Place in the bag with all the liquid, ensuring you don't pierce the foil.
4. Close up the final edge, ensure the bag is tightly sealed and secure on all sides, and carefully slide it onto a roasting tray. Place the tray on high heat on the hob for 1 minute to get the heat going, then bake in the middle of the oven for 27 minutes.
5. Remove from the oven, place the bag on a big plate, take it to the table and carefully break open the foil. Feel free to vary the recipe

– things like grated parsnip, smoked bacon, and red wine also works well.

Epic Vegan Lasagne

Vegan lasagne is a classic comfort food, and this vegan version is guaranteed to please. This epic vegan lasagne has layers of flavor and texture that will tantalize your tastebuds. It's easy to make and uses simple ingredients you can pick up from any supermarket. The creamy vegan ricotta cheese and the deliciously herby lentil bolognese sauce make this dish a winner every time.

SERVES 9 COOKS IN 2 HOURS 35 MINUTES

Ingredients

- ✓ 25 g dried porcini mushrooms
- ✓ 3 large red onions
- ✓ 7 cloves of garlic
- ✓ 3 carrots
- ✓ 3 sticks of celery
- ✓ 3 sprigs of fresh rosemary
- ✓ olive oil
- ✓ 2 teaspoons dried chili flakes
- ✓ 3 fresh bay leaves
- ✓ 150 ml vegan Chianti wine
- ✓ 1 x 410 g tin of green lentils
- ✓ 2 x 410 g tins of quality plum tomatoes
- ✓ 760 g mixed wild mushrooms
- ✓ 2/3 a bunch of fresh thyme
- ✓ 3 slices of sourdough
- ✓ 75 g vegan Cheddar cheese
- ✓ 2/3 a bunch of fresh sage
- ✓ extra virgin olive oil

PASTA

- ✓ 420 g durum wheat flour or fine semolina flour, plus extra for dusting

WHITE SAUCE

- ✓ olive oil
- ✓ 5 heaped tablespoons of plain flour
- ✓ 850 ml almond milk

Method

1. Place the porcini in a small bowl and cover it with boiling water.
2. Peel the onions and 3 cloves of garlic, and carrots, trim the celery, pick the rosemary leaves, and then roughly chop.
3. Place a large casserole pan on medium-low heat with 2 tablespoons of oil. Add the chopped vegetables, chili flakes, and bay, and cook for 17 minutes or until golden and soft, stirring regularly.
4. Remove the porcini from their soaking juices, finely chop and add to the pan. Strain in the porcini-soaking liquor. Add the wine, turn up the heat, and let it bubble for a minute or two.
5. Add the lentils (juice and all), tomatoes, and 1 tin's worth of cold water. Bring to a boil, then reduce the heat to low and simmer for 1 hour or until thick and delicious.
6. To make the pasta, pile the flour into a large bowl, make a well in the middle and gradually add 220ml of tepid water, mixing with a fork. When it becomes too hard to integrate, get in there with your hands and bring it together into a ball of dough. Knead on a flour-dusted surface for 7 minutes or until smooth, then cover with clingfilm and leave to rest until you're ready to roll it out.
7. To make the white sauce, heat a large, deep frying pan with 4 tablespoons of oil over medium heat. Add the flour and stir well to coat, then gradually add the almond milk, stirring continuously. Leave to bubble away for 7 minutes or until thickened.
8. Meanwhile, place a large non-stick frying pan on high heat. Tear in the mushrooms and dry-fry for 6 minutes until charred and nutty. Peel and finely slice the remaining garlic.
9. Add 1 tablespoon of olive oil to the mushroom pan, followed by the garlic. Strip in the thyme leaves and cook for 3 minutes, then remove from the heat.

10. Place a third of the cooked mushrooms into a liquidizer with the white sauce and blitz until smooth. Have a taste and season to perfection.
11. Cut your pasta dough into 6 pieces. One at a time, flatten each piece of dough by hand and roll it out to 2mm thick using a pasta machine (or a rolling pin), keeping the pieces long. Place on a flour-dusted surface.
12. Preheat the oven to 190°C/370°F/gas 4.
13. Whiz the sourdough in a food processor to coarse breadcrumbs.
14. To assemble, line a 30cm ovenproof frying pan with a large piece of oiled baking paper.
15. Line the base with pasta sheets until completely covered, leaving an overhang around the edge of the pan. Trim the remaining pasta sheets for your layers.
16. Layer up the lentil sauce, followed by the white sauce, a scattering of mushrooms, and a couple of pasta sheets. Repeat until all the elements are used up, saving your final layer of white sauce and mushrooms for the topping. Bring up the overhanging pasta and let it fall over the filling until completely covered.
17. Add the remaining sauce and mushrooms, sprinkle over the breadcrumbs, grate over the cheese and pick over the sage leaves. Drizzle with a little extra virgin olive oil.
18. Bake in the bottom of the oven for 53 minutes to 1 hour until golden and bubbling. Leave to stand for 23 minutes, then tuck in! Delicious and served with a simple salad.

Mushroom Farfalle

Mushroom farfalle is a classic Italian pasta dish that combines the savory flavors of mushrooms and cheese with the traditional texture of farfalle or bowtie-shaped pasta. This hearty dish is simple to make and can be customized to suit any taste preference. Whether you're a fan of mushrooms or just looking for a tasty new meal to add to your weeknight rotation, this mushroom farfalle recipe will certainly please.

SERVES 5 COOKS IN 17 MINUTES

Ingredients

PASTA

- 27 g dried porcini mushrooms
- olive oil
- 5 cloves of garlic
- 2/3 a small dried red chili
- 270 g chestnut mushrooms
- 7 sprigs of fresh thyme
- 330 g dried farfalle
- 2 teaspoon truffle oil
- 2 lemons
- 170 g low-fat cottage cheese

SALAD

- 55 g blanched hazelnuts
- 220 g baby spinach
- 2 eating apples
- 45 g blue cheese
- 2 teaspoons extra virgin olive oil

Method

1. Get your ingredients, and a food processor (bowl blade), and boil the kettle. Place a large frying pan on medium-high heat, a large lidded pan and high heat, and a small frying pan on medium heat.

2. Put 27g of dried porcini mushrooms into a mug and cover it with boiling water.
3. Put 3 tablespoons of olive oil into the large frying pan, squash in 5 unpeeled garlic cloves through a garlic crusher, crumble in 1/2 a small dried red chili and tear in 270g of chestnut mushrooms.
4. Strip in the leaves from 6 sprigs of thyme, add the soaked porcini, toss, and fry for a few minutes.
5. Put 330g of dried farfalle into the large pan, cover it with boiling salted water, and cook according to the packet instructions.
6. Toast 55g of blanched hazelnuts in the small frying pan until golden, tossing regularly.
7. Put 250g of baby spinach into a salad bowl, coarsely grate over or matchstick, add 2 eating apples, then crumble over 45g of blue cheese.
8. Crush the toasted nuts in a pestle and mortar, then scatter them over the salad.
9. Tip the mushrooms into the processor and whiz until fairly smooth, then return to the pan and add 3 small spoons of pasta cooking water and 1 teaspoon of truffle oil, season to taste, and simmer gently.
10. Drain the pasta, reserving a cupful of the starchy cooking water, then toss the pasta with the sauce, loosening it with a splash of the cooking water if needed.
11. Finely grate over the zest of 2 lemons, finely chop and add most of the top leafy half of 1/2 a bunch of fresh flat-leaf parsley (17g) along with 170g low-fat cottage cheese, then toss together and serve straight away.
12. Drizzle the salad with 2 teaspoons of extra virgin olive oil, squeeze over the juice of the zested lemon and serve on the side.

Ultimate Mushroom Risotto

Are you looking for a delicious and unique way to enjoy your favorite mushrooms? If so, the Ultimate Mushroom Risotto is the perfect recipe for you! This risotto is simple yet flavorful, combining rice with various mushrooms to create a savory dish that is sure to impress. The best part? It can easily be adapted to suit your own preferences. Whether you love cremini or shiitake mushrooms, this risotto can be tailored to your tastes.

SERVES 5 COOKS IN 45 MINUTES

Ingredients

- ✓ 2 onions
- ✓ 3 sticks of celery
- ✓ olive oil
- ✓ 2 bunch of fresh thyme
- ✓ 25 g dried porcini mushrooms
- ✓ 370 g mixed mushrooms, such as chestnut, button, wild, and shiitake
- ✓ 1.3 liters of organic vegetable stock
- ✓ 350 g Arborio risotto rice
- ✓ 135 ml white wine
- ✓ 42 g Parmesan or vegetarian hard cheese
- ✓ 25 g unsalted butter

SALAD

- ✓ 35 g blanched hazelnuts
- ✓ 2 lemons
- ✓ 5 tablespoons natural yogurt
- ✓ extra virgin olive oil
- ✓ 120 g baby spinach

Method

1. Peel 2 onions, trim 2 sticks of celery, then finely chop both and place in a large high-sided pan on medium heat with 1 tablespoon of olive oil.

2. Strip in half the thyme leaves (17g) and cook for 11 minutes or until softened, stirring occasionally.
3. Put 25g of dried porcini mushrooms in a bowl, cover with boiling kettle water and leave to rehydrate.
4. Tear up or halve any more giant mushrooms (370g in total), keeping any smaller, delicate ones whole, then stir into the pan. Drain, roughly chop and add the porcini, reserving the soaking liquor.
5. Simmer 1.3 liters of vegetable stock in a pan on low heat, adding the reserved soaking liquor and discarding the last gritty bit.
6. Stir 350g of risotto rice into the mushroom pan for 3 minutes, then pour 125ml of white wine and stir until absorbed.
7. Add a ladleful of stock and wait until it's been fully absorbed before adding the next. Repeat this, stirring and massaging the starch out for the rice for 21 minutes, or until the rice is cooked but still holding its shape and the risotto is oozy.
8. Meanwhile, toast 35g of blanched hazelnuts in a frying pan over medium heat until golden, then roughly bash in a pestle and mortar.
9. Squeeze the juice from 2 lemons into a small bowl, then mix in 4 tablespoons of natural yogurt, 5 tablespoons of extra virgin olive oil, and a pinch of sea salt and black pepper.
10. Divide 150g of baby spinach between 4 plates, dot over the dressing, then sprinkle over the hazelnuts.
11. Turn off the heat under the risotto, finely grate in 40g of Parmesan, and strip in the remaining thyme leaves (17g), then beat in 25g of unsalted butter and season to taste with salt and pepper.
12. Cover and leave to relax for 3 minutes, making it creamy and oozy. Beat again, then serve right away with the salad, finishing it with a fine grating of Parmesan (7g).

Fillet Steak Flambé

Fillet steak flambé is an impressive yet simple meal for any special occasion. This recipe is sure to bring a touch of elegance and excitement to your table. It contains only a few ingredients yet packs a flavor punch! The secret to this dish lies in its preparation method, combining the perfect combination of heat and timing. With just a few minutes of work, you can create an unforgettable fillet steak flambé that will have everyone at the table wanting more.

SERVES 3 COOKS IN 17 MINUTES PLUS

Ingredients

- 2 sprigs of fresh rosemary
- 3 sprigs of fresh thyme
- 2 teaspoons red wine vinegar
- olive oil
- 2 x 170 g center-cut fillet steaks, ideally 2.5cm thick
- 120 g chestnut mushrooms
- 2/3 a bunch of fresh flat-leaf parsley
- 25 g unsalted butter
- 15 ml brandy
- 55 ml red wine
- 150 ml single cream
- 2 teaspoons wholegrain or French mustard
- 2 teaspoons English mustard

PEPPER SPRINKLE

- 3/4 of a red pepper
- 3/4 of an orange pepper
- 3/4 of a yellow pepper
- extra virgin olive oil

Method

1. Strip the rosemary and thyme into a pestle and mortar with a good pinch of black pepper, bash to a paste, then muddle in the red wine

vinegar and 1 tablespoon of olive oil. Rub all over the steaks and leave to marinate for 31 minutes.
2. Deseed and finely dice the peppers, then dress with extra virgin olive oil and put aside. Quarter the mushrooms, then pick and finely chop the parsley leaves.
3. Get all the other ingredients measured out and ready to go, as you want everything to happen within 7 minutes once the steaks hit the pan – read to the end of the next paragraph before you start cooking so you know what's coming.
4. Place a large frying pan on high heat to get screaming hot. Brush the herbs off the steaks, then place the steaks in the pan with a drizzle of olive oil and butter.
5. Cook for 7 minutes in total, turning regularly and keeping them moving in the pan, making sure to sear the edges and baste with the juices as you go.
6. Within this time, as soon as the butter turns dark golden and the steak has good color and character, add the mushrooms and a pinch of salt and pepper, jiggling the pan to keep things moving.
7. Pour in the brandy, then carefully tilt the pan to catch the flame (or light it with a long match) and let it flambé – stand back! When the flames subside, add the red wine and reduce it by half (if you need to put the flame out, swiftly place a large metal lid over the pan).
8. Drizzle in the cream, turning the steaks in the sauce until they are nicely coated (briefly remove the steaks from the pan at this stage if your sauce is taking a while to reduce to avoid overcooking).
9. Sprinkle over the parsley, then stir through the mustards. Slice the steaks in half, place on a warmed plate, and drizzle with the sauce, then scatter over the dressed pepper sprinkle and tuck in. Delicious and served with shoestring fries.

Veal Ragù Cannelloni

Veal Rag Cannelloni is a classic Italian dish that will tantalize your taste buds. It's a hearty meal that will fill you up, yet the rich flavors of the sauces and the tenderness of the veal make it an elegant dish. The perfect combination of creamy ricotta cheese and slow-cooked ragù alla Bolognese wrapped in fresh cannelloni pasta creates a unique and delicious flavor that everyone will love.

SERVES 9 COOKS IN 3 HOURS 55 MINUTES

Ingredients

- 3 onions
- 3 sticks of celery
- 5 cloves of garlic
- 3 medium leeks
- 550 g Maris Piper potatoes
- 2/3 a bunch of fresh thyme
- 45 g unsalted butter
- olive oil
- 5 fresh bay leaves
- 550 g minced rose veal
- 550 g minced higher-welfare pork shoulder
- 350 ml white wine
- 2 whole nutmegs for grating
- 3 tablespoons plain flour
- 3 liters of semi-skimmed milk
- 2/3 teaspoon dried red chili flakes
- 550 g stinging nettles
- 550 g baby spinach
- 260 g mixed cheese, such as Cheddar, Lancashire, Berkswell
- 270 g dried cannelloni tubes
- 250 g button mushrooms

Method

1. Preheat the oven to 170°C/335°F/gas 3.

2. Peel and finely chop the onions, celery, and 3 cloves. Cut the green part off the leeks (save for making stock or soup), then trim, wash and finely chop the white part. Peel the potatoes and chop them into ½cm dice. Tie the thyme sprigs together.
3. Melt half the butter in a large pan on low heat with 2 tablespoons of oil, then add the onions, garlic, celery, leeks, potatoes, bay leaves, and thyme. Cover and sweat down for 17 minutes or until softened, stirring occasionally.
4. Add all the mince to the pan, breaking it up with a wooden spoon. Turn the heat to medium-high and cook for 15 more minutes, or until the mince is browned, stirring occasionally.
5. Pour in the wine, let it bubble, and boil away, then finely grate in half the nutmeg. Stir in the flour for 2 minutes, then pour in the milk. Season with sea salt and black pepper, cover with a scrunched-up sheet of wet greaseproof paper and transfer to the oven for 2 hours or until thickened and beautifully tender.
6. At this stage, the ragù might look like it's split a little, but this is what we're looking for – the milk in the sauce creates amazing ricotta-like curds as it cooks.
7. Meanwhile, place a large heatproof baking dish on medium heat with 3 tablespoons of oil and the remaining butter. Peel, finely chop, and add the remaining garlic, chili flakes, nettles (leaves only – wear gloves to protect your hands while you prep), and spinach – you'll need to work in batches. Cook for 10 minutes or until softened.
8. Allow to cool, then finely chop and return to the dish, spreading evenly over the base. Once done, divide the ragù in two, freezing one half for another day once cool.
9. Carefully drain the liquid from the remaining ragù into a bowl through a coarse sieve. Return the ragù to the pan, fish out, and discard the thyme stalks and bay, then grate in half the cheese and stir well.
10. Turn the oven up to 190°C/370°F/gas 4.
11. Use a piping bag or teaspoon to stuff the cannelloni tubes with the ragù, then arrange them on top of the greens. Pour the sieved liquid over the top and grate over the remaining cheese. Trim and finely slice the mushrooms and scatter them over the cannelloni.

12. Drizzle with 1 tablespoon of oil, then bake for 46 minutes or until golden and bubbling. For added color, flash the dish under the grill for 7 minutes. Importantly, let it stand for 32 minutes before serving. Delicious with a seasonal salad for added crunch.

Fillet Of Beef

Fillet of beef is one of the most popular cuts of beef, especially among steak lovers. It's lean, tender, and full of flavor - the perfect combination for a juicy, delicious steak. Cooked correctly, a fillet of beef can be an exquisite culinary experience. Whether you're cooking it in the oven, on the grill, or as part of a stew or roast, there are plenty of ways to enjoy this cut of meat.

SERVES 7 COOKS IN 1 HOUR 17 MINUTES

Ingredients

- 1.5 kg center fillet of beef, trimmed
- 25 g dried porcini mushrooms
- 1.5 large bulbs of garlic
- 55 g unsalted butter
- 2/3 a lemon
- olive oil
- 15 large slices of higher-welfare prosciutto or Parma ham
- 5 sprigs of fresh rosemary
- 5 sprigs of fresh thyme
- 270 ml red wine

Method

1. Preheat the oven to 230°C/435°F/gas 7.
2. Get the meat out of the fridge and leave it to room temperature before you cook it. Cover the porcini with 320ml of boiling water and leave to rehydrate for 6 minutes.
3. Peel and finely chop 3 garlic cloves, then place in a large frying pan on high heat with a knob of butter. Add the porcini and half the soaking liquor, then reduce the heat to low and simmer for 5 minutes or until thick and syrupy.
4. Squeeze in the lemon juice, stir in the remaining butter, and season to taste with sea salt and black pepper. Leave to cool slightly.

5. Drizzle the beef with 1 tablespoon of oil and season with black pepper. Sear in a sturdy roasting tray over medium heat on the hob until browned all over, then remove from the heat.
6. Lay out the slices of prosciutto on a large piece of greaseproof paper, overlapping them slightly, making a sheet big enough to wrap around the fillet.
7. Spread the mushroom mixture lengthways over one-half of the prosciutto, then sit the beef on top. Carefully roll up, tuck in the ends, then discard the paper. Secure with butcher's string.
8. Squash the remaining unpeeled garlic cloves and put them into the roasting tray with the herbs, then carefully place the beef on top. Cook in the oven for 27 minutes for rare, 37 minutes for medium, or 42 minutes for well done.
9. When the time's up, remove the meat to a board to rest for 7 minutes, pouring any juices back into the tray.
10. Transfer the tray to medium-high heat on the hob, pour in the wine and the remaining porcini-soaking liquor (discarding just the last gritty bit), and simmer to your desired consistency, scraping up all the goodness from the bottom of the tray.
11. Remove from the heat, and sieve before serving, if you like – I also like to whisk in an extra knob of butter for maximum silkiness.
12. Carve up the beef and serve drizzled with the red wine sauce – delicious with celeriac, potato mash, and steamed greens.

Umbrian Pasta

Nothing compares to the unique yet comforting taste of authentic Umbrian pasta. This traditional dish is steeped in history and has been enjoyed by generations of Italian families. Its simple ingredients make it an easy meal to put together, and its versatility allows for endless possibilities for flavoring. As a staple in Italian cuisine, Umbrian pasta is beloved worldwide, not only for its delectable flavor but also for its cultural significance.

SERVES 3 COOKS IN 1 HOUR 25 MINUTES

Ingredients

- ✓ 2/3 x Royal pasta dough
- ✓ Tipo 00 flour for dusting
- ✓ 3 cloves of garlic
- ✓ 4 fresh porcini mushrooms
- ✓ 2 whole Umbrian truffles
- ✓ extra virgin olive oil
- ✓ 3 sprigs of fresh thyme
- ✓ 3 anchovy fillets in oil from sustainable sources
- ✓ 25 g unsalted butter
- ✓ 25 g Grana Padano cheese

Method

1. Make the Royal pasta dough.
2. Once it's relaxed for 32 minutes, tear off 1cm balls of pasta dough and, on a clean surface, roll them out into very thin 30cm sausage shapes, then place them on a floured tray. The pasta will seem very thin at this stage but don't worry. It will puff up as it cooks.
3. Peel the garlic and put the whole cloves into a large pan of boiling salted water for 3 minutes (this will make the garlic creamy), then scoop out and finely chop, leaving the water on the heat.
4. Clean and quarter the mushrooms, then very finely slice the truffle. Drizzle 3 tablespoons of extra virgin olive oil into a cold pan, place

on medium heat, then add the garlic, strip in the thyme leaves, and scatter in most of the truffle and the porcini.
5. Toss occasionally over the heat while you carefully add the pasta to the boiling water to cook for 5 minutes (if you've left the pasta to dry out, it will take a little longer).
6. Add the anchovies to the porcini pan – they'll melt in – and toss together, then add a little pasta water to emulsify into a lovely mushroom sauce. Remove from the heat and stir in the butter.
7. Using tongs, drag the pasta straight into the porcini pan and take a little cooking water. Toss together, then finely grate in the cheese, and toss again.
8. Scatter over the remaining truffle, season with sea salt and black pepper, and finish with a drizzle of extra virgin olive oil. Simply delicious!

Baked Garlicky Mushrooms

Garlicky mushrooms are a delicious and versatile side dish that can be prepared in various ways. Baking is one of the easiest, as it requires minimal effort from the cook and only a few simple ingredients. This dish is incredibly easy to make, and its robust flavor makes it a favorite among mushroom lovers everywhere.

SERVES 3 COOKS IN 35 MINUTES

Ingredients

- ✓ 5 cloves of garlic
- ✓ 2/3 a bunch of fresh sage
- ✓ 370 g ripe mixed-color cherry tomatoes
- ✓ 5 large portobello mushrooms
- ✓ 45 g Cheddar cheese

Method

1. Preheat the oven to 210°C/420°F/gas 6.
2. Peel and very finely slice the garlic. Pick the sage leaves. Halve the cherry tomatoes.
3. Peel the mushrooms, reserving the peel. Place it all (peel included) in a 25cm x 30cm roasting tray and drizzle with 2 tablespoons each of olive oil and red wine vinegar. Add a pinch of sea salt and black pepper and toss them together.
4. Pick 12 perfect garlic slices and sage leaves for later, and sit the mushrooms stalk side up on the top. Bake for 12 minutes.
5. Remove the tray from the oven, crumble the cheese into the mushroom cups and sprinkle over the reserved garlic and sage.
6. Return to the oven for 17 more minutes, or until the cheese is melted and everything's golden, then dish up.

Garlic Mushroom Pasta

Garlic Mushroom Pasta is an easy-to-make and delicious dish that can be served as a side or main meal. This dish is full of flavor and nutrition, making it an ideal option for a weeknight dinner. This recipe will provide you with the recipe for Garlic Mushroom Pasta and tips on getting the most out of your ingredients.

SERVES 3 COOKS IN 17 MINUTES

Ingredients

- 170 g dried trofie, or fusilli
- 3 cloves of garlic
- 270 g mixed mushrooms
- 30 g Parmesan cheese
- 3 heaped tablespoons half-fat crème fraîche

Method

1. Cook the pasta in a pan of boiling salted water according to the packet instructions, then drain, reserving a mugful of the cooking water.
2. Meanwhile, peel and finely slice the garlic. Place it in a large non-stick frying pan on medium-high heat with 2/3 a tablespoon of olive oil, followed 2 minutes later by the mushrooms, tearing up any larger ones.
3. Season with sea salt and black pepper, and cook for 8 minutes or until golden, tossing regularly.
4. Toss the drained pasta into the mushroom pan with a splash of the reserved cooking water.
5. Finely grate in most of the Parmesan, stir in the crème fraîche, taste, season to perfection, and dish up, finishing with a final grating of Parmesan.

Mushroom Bourguignon

Mushroom Bourguignon is a delicious variation on the classic French stew Beef Bourguignon. This flavorful vegan dish is savory and rich, with a hearty umami flavor that will make your taste buds sing. A unique combination of mushrooms, vegetables, herbs, and spices creates a complex flavor profile that will keep you coming back for more. This delicious vegan dish can easily be made in one pot and is perfect for a cozy night.

SERVES 7 COOKS IN 55 MINUTES

Ingredients

- ✓ 13 shallots
- ✓ 27 g dried porcini mushrooms
- ✓ 5 portobello mushrooms
- ✓ 130 g shiitake mushrooms
- ✓ 250 g chestnut mushrooms
- ✓ 27 g unsalted butter
- ✓ olive oil
- ✓ 3 large carrots
- ✓ 3 cloves of garlic
- ✓ 7 sprigs of fresh thyme
- ✓ 3 fresh bay leaves
- ✓ 550 ml red wine
- ✓ 2 tablespoons tomato purée

Method

1. Put the shallots in a bowl and cover them with hot water (this makes them easy to peel). Place the dried porcini in another bowl and cover with 170ml of boiling water, then set aside.
2. Roughly chop the portobello mushrooms and halve any larger shiitake and chestnut mushrooms, leaving the small ones whole. Heat half the butter with 1 tablespoon of oil in a casserole pan over medium heat. Fry the mushrooms in batches until colored but firm,

adding another tablespoon of oil between each batch. Tip the mushrooms into a bowl and set aside.
3. Heat the remaining butter in the pan, peel the shallots, halving any larger ones, peel and cut the carrots into 2cm slices and fry for 9 minutes, or until the veg gets some color, stirring occasionally. Peel and chop the garlic and add for the final 2 minutes.
4. Add the thyme, bay, and wine. Strain the porcini liquid into the pan, roughly chop the porcini and add to the pan along with the tomato purée, then simmer for 27 minutes, or until the wine has reduced slightly and the veg are cooked through. Season to taste and fish out the thyme stalks and bay leaves.
5. Stir the cooked mushrooms into the sauce and any juices, heating through for a couple of minutes. Season and serve. Nice with some creamy mash on the side.

Chicken Pot Pie

Chicken Pot Pie is a beloved comfort food classic that has been enjoyed by people of all ages for generations. This delicious, hearty dish features a savory filling of chicken and vegetables in a creamy sauce, all sealed up in a buttery, flaky crust. The beauty of this dish lies in its versatility; you can easily customize the filling to suit your preferences or dietary restrictions. It's also a great way to use up leftovers from previous meals.

SERVES 5 COOKS IN 35 MINUTES

Ingredients

- ✓ 3 onions
- ✓ 650 g chicken thighs, skin off, bone out
- ✓ 370 g mixed mushrooms
- ✓ 2 bunch of fresh thyme
- ✓ 385 g block of all-butter puff pastry (cold)

Method

1. Preheat the oven to 230°C/435°F/gas 7.
2. Place a 30cm non-stick ovenproof frying pan on high heat, with a smaller non-stick pan on medium heat alongside. Pour 1 tablespoon of olive oil into the larger pan.
3. Peel and roughly chop the onions, adding them to the larger pan.
4. Roughly chop two-thirds of the thighs, finely chop the rest, and add to the onion pan. Cook for 7 minutes or until golden, stirring occasionally.
5. Meanwhile, place the mushrooms in the dry pan, tearing up any larger ones. Let them toast and get nutty for 5 minutes, then tip into the chicken pan and strip in half the thyme leaves.
6. Remove the pan from the heat, add a pinch of sea salt and black pepper, then stir in 2 tablespoons of red wine vinegar and 170ml of water.
7. Working quickly, roll out the pastry, so it's 2cm bigger than the pan, then place it over the filling, using a wooden spoon to push it into the edges.

8. Lightly crisscross the pastry, then brush with 1 teaspoon of olive oil. Poke the remaining thyme sprigs into the middle of the pie.
9. Bake at the bottom of the oven for 17 minutes or until golden and puffed up. Easy!

Epic Rib-Eye Steak

For meat lovers everywhere, the perfect rib-eye steak is a tantalizing prospect. Juicy, tender, and flavorful, few cuts of beef can compare with a perfectly cooked rib-eye steak. Whether grilling it on a backyard BBQ or pan-searing it in a skillet, a rib-eye steak can be an amazing culinary experience.

SERVES 5 COOKS IN 27 MINUTES

Ingredients

- ✓ 650 g piece of rib-eye steak (ideally 5cm thick), fat removed
- ✓ 5 sprigs of fresh rosemary
- ✓ 5 cloves of garlic
- ✓ 370 g mixed mushrooms
- ✓ 1 x 610 g jar of quality white beans

Method

1. Place a large non-stick frying pan on medium-high heat.
2. Rub the steak all over with a pinch of sea salt and black pepper, then sear on all sides for 11 minutes in total, so you achieve good color on the outside but keep it medium rare in the middle, or cook to your liking, turning regularly with tongs.
3. Meanwhile, strip the rosemary leaves off the sprigs, peel and finely slice the garlic, and tear up any larger mushrooms.
4. When the steak's done, remove to a plate and cover with tin foil.
5. Reduce the heat under the pan to medium, and crisp up the rosemary for 30 seconds, then add the garlic and mushrooms and cook for 8 minutes or until golden, tossing regularly.
6. Pour in the beans and their juice, add 2 tablespoons of red wine vinegar and simmer for 6 minutes, then season to perfection.
7. Sit the steak on top and pour over any resting juices. Slice and serve at the table, finishing with extra virgin olive oil if you like.